W9-CKD-486
IT'S HIT THE END OF ITS LIFESPAN, THAT'S ALL.
FORTY-FOUR YEARS AFTER THE END OF THE VALBANILL WAR.
IS THERE ANY WAY YOU COULD REFORGE IT?
I'M AFRAID NOT.
WE'VE JUST CRACKED THE MOLDS ON SOME NEW SWORDS. HOW ABOUT ONE OF THOSE?
"HOUSMAN" — ONE OF THE INDEPENDENT TRADE CITIES.
CHING
NO, THANKS.
THIS BLADE IS AN HEIRLOOM FROM MY FATHER, AND HIS FATHER BEFORE HIM. IT IS MY HEART MADE STEEL.

WITHDRAWN

There was once a horrific war that made full use of the Demon Pact on a continent. And it is—now.
SO WHEN I GO TO BATTLE, I WANT NONE OTHER THAN THIS BLADE IN MY HANDS.

KRUNCH
WHOOSH
WHY ME?! WHY ALWAYS ME?!!
WHY WON'T ANYONE EVER HELP ME?!!
PERSE-CUTED! HUNTED!!
YOU THERE! WHAT DO YOU THINK YOU'RE DOING?!
FREEZE
TIP TIP TIP
LOOKS TO ME LIKE SOME VAGRANT'S GONE CRAZY.
SAY, WHAT'S GOING ON OVER THERE?

SKSHHH
TMP
TMP
TMP
TMP
TMP
MY NAME IS CECILY CAMPBELL!
I AM A MEMBER OF THE INDEPENDENT TRADE CITIES' KNIGHT GUARD, THIRD DISTRICT CORPS!!
SHIIING

PUT DOWN YOUR WEAPON, AND TURN TOWARDS ME CALMLY!
!
RELAX, CECILY. HE'S ONLY A CRAZY OLD MAN. NOTHING TO GET WORKED UP OVER.
HUPPP
HUPPP
THAT DOESN'T LOOK LIKE AN ORDINARY WOUND...
HIS HAND!
WHYY-YYYYY ??!!!
ビク
SHUDDER

KLANG
!!
CEASE THIS, YOU--
OH GODS!
HURRRR
HURRRR

WH-WHO IS THIS MAN?
AND WHAT ON EARTH IS WRONG WITH HIM?!
NH ...!
WHOOSH
KAAA
KAAA
ARGH! ENOUGH, CECILY CAMPBELL, THIS IS PATHETIC!
HALF THE CITY IS STANDING HERE, WATCHING YOU!!
S-SO THIS IS WHAT IT'S LIKE TO BE IN A REAL FIGHT...
SHVR
SHVR
HAAH ...
HAAH ...
HAAAAAH!!
SWOOSH
STOP BEING SUCH A COWARD!!

HUH...?

THUNK
IT...
IT BROKE...!
THE ANCESTRAL BLADE OF THE VENERABLE HOUSE CAMPBELL JUST BROKE!
HRAAAAAAH!!
FWOOSH

I'VE BEEN A KNIGHT FOR JUST ONE MONTH.
YES, THIS IS THE FIRST TRUE FIGHT I HAVE EVER BEEN IN, BUT TO BE THIS HELPLESS...?
THIS IS TURNING OUT TO BE A PAINFUL LESSON IN MY OWN SHORT-COMINGS.
FWISH

FWISH
?!

A BLADE.
IN A SHAPE I'VE NEVER SEEN BEFORE.
IT'S BEAUTIFUL...!

YOU HAVE MADE "DEMON PACTS," THEN.
A PITIFUL "VETERAN" OF THE WAR. UNABLE TO HOLD A JOB OR EVEN ADJUST TO NORMAL LIFE, YOU'VE LOST SIGHT OF ANY REASON TO LIVE AND HAVE GIVEN IN TO DESPAIR. AM I CORRECT?
I SEE YOU ARE MISSING FINGERS ON YOUR HAND.
URK...
!!!HRRRA
WAAA
WAIT!
AH!
THUNK

THAT DULL GLEAM OFF HIS LEFT EYE... IS IT GLASS?
THANK YOU FOR HELPING ME--
--EE...
EEP!
?!
HUH?
SPLAAAT
ACK !!
MY... MY KNEES COLLAPSED ON ME!
HEH HEH HEH...

LUKE, YOU SHOULDN'T LAUGH LIKE THAT!
SH-SHUT UP!!
HA HA HA HA!
WELL, AREN'T YOU THE BATTLE-HARDENED KNIGHT.
REALLY?
LISA, COME. WE STILL HAVE TO MAKE OUR DELIVERY.
AH...! ARE YOU OKAY, MISS?
TP TP
UM...
OH...
ERM, YES. THANK YOU.

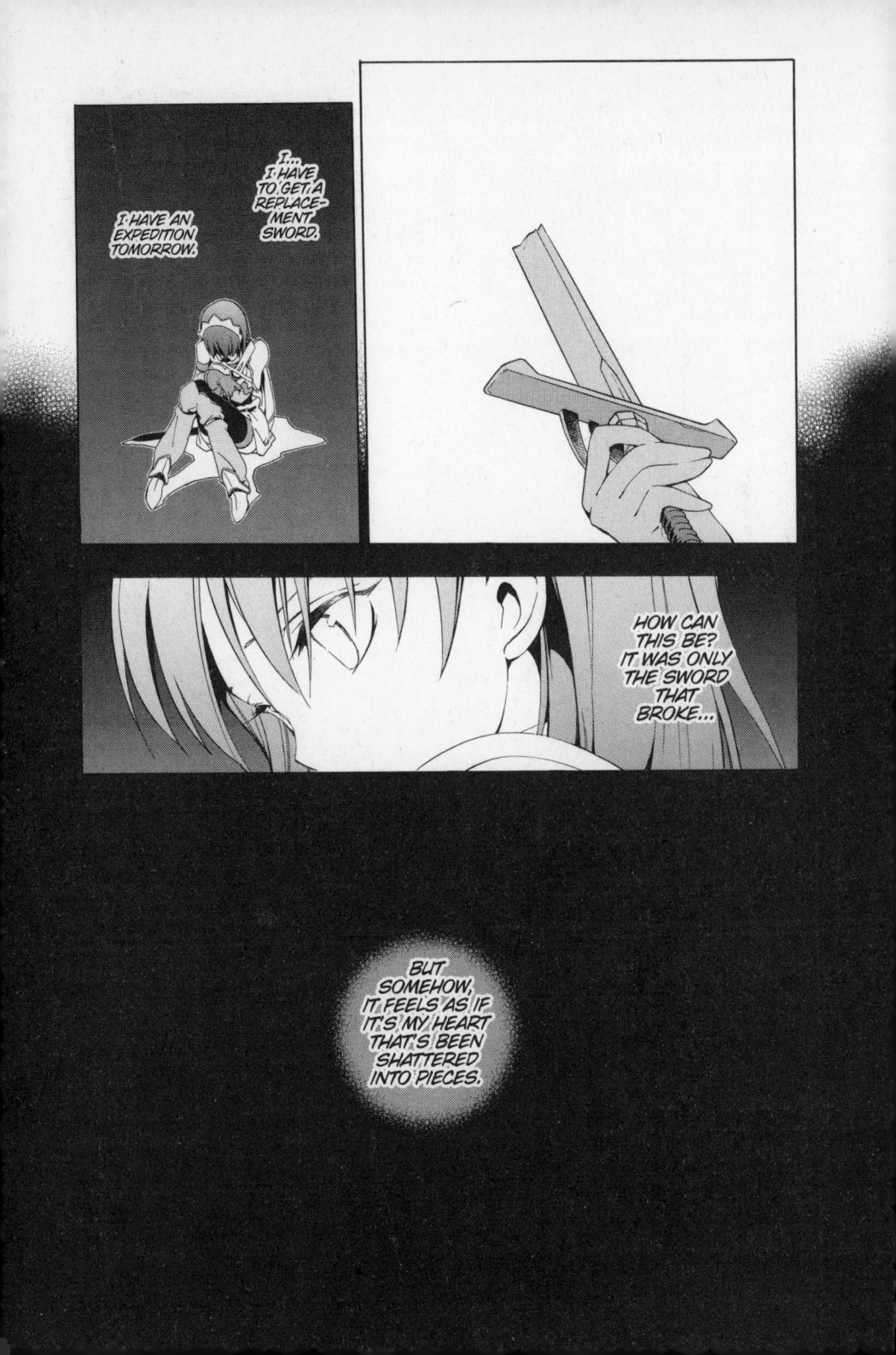
I HAVE AN EXPEDITION TOMORROW.
I... I HAVE TO GET A REPLACEMENT SWORD.
HOW CAN THIS BE? IT WAS ONLY THE SWORD THAT BROKE...
BUT SOMEHOW, IT FEELS AS IF IT'S MY HEART THAT'S BEEN SHATTERED INTO PIECES.

A BLADE THAT CAN SLICE THROUGH IRON.
IT MAY BE OF A SHAPE THAT I HAVE NEVER SEEN BEFORE...
BUT THERE IS NO DOUBTING ITS POWER. IT MUST'VE BEEN MADE AT THE HAND OF A VERY FAMOUS BLACKSMITH.
YOU MEAN LUKE'S SWORD?
OH, HE FORGED THAT ALL BY HIMSELF.
IT'S SUPPOSED TO BE A SECRET, THOUGH!
WHAT?!

YEP! WE RUN A LITTLE SMITHY, MAKING AND REPAIRING EVERYDAY ITEMS ON THE EDGE OF THE SEVENTH DISTRICT.
IT'S CALLED ATELIER LIZA!
THAT BLADE...

I MUST HAVE ONE!!

Forty-four years after the close of the Valbanill War—
The Empire, the Crowd Powers, and the Militant Nation have all withdrawn, segregating themselves from each other.
And so, the continent entered an age of peace.

Tucked away in a corner of the continent, one of the independent Trade Cities, "Housman."

IT IS IN A SMALL SMITHY AT THE EDGE OF THIS CITY THAT OUR STORY BEGINS...

Chapter 1 Knight (Part 1)

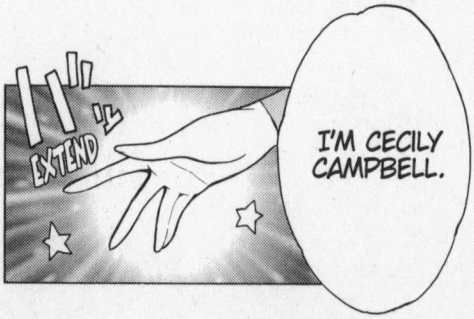

SILENCE
GRAB
?!
PROPER GREETINGS ARE IMPORTANT!
IT'S NICE TO MEET YOU!
SHAKE
SHAKE
ST-STOP THAT!
AND WHY DID YOU FOLLOW ME?
I HEARD THIS WAS A SMITHY.
I WOULD LIKE TO PLACE AN ORDER.
OH. A CUSTOMER, EH?

BABAAAM!!!
IS A SWORD, JUST LIKE YOURS!
SICKLE
KAMA
WHAT WOULD YOU LIKE?
SCISSORS
HASAMI
I TAKE ORDERS FOR EVERYDAY ITEMS ONLY.
HATCHET
NATA
HOE
KUWA
WHAT I WOULD LIKE YOU TO MAKE FOR ME...
!
SORRY. THIS SMITHY CEASED MAKING WEAPONS WITH MY FATHER'S GENERATION.
WHAT?
IF YOU WANT A BLADE, GO ELSE-WHERE.

WH-WHY?! THAT BLADE YOU WORE IN THE CITY WAS ONE YOU FORGED YOURSELF, WAS IT NOT?
!
LISA TOLD ME SO!
YEEP!!
TWITCH
GLARE
WOULD ANYONE CARE FOR SOME TEA? ♪
LISA!
YOU OBVIOUSLY HAVE AN INCREDIBLE TALENT FOR IT... WHY HIDE IT?
SOMEONE OF YOUR SKILL CAN'T BE UNAWARE, LUKE.
YOU HAVE TO KNOW JUST HOW POWERFUL THE BLADE YOU MADE IS.
GO HOME.

"KATANA."
SO THAT'S WHAT THAT CURVED BLADE IS CALLED.

I FORGE KATANA FOR MY OWN USE ONLY.

NO EXCEP-TIONS.

THAT IS SOMETHING I MADE UP MY MIND ABOUT, A LONG TIME AGO.

LUKE...?
I KNOW I'M ACTING VERY CONFIDENT ABOUT ALL THIS, BUT TO BE HONEST, I'VE ONLY BEEN A KNIGHT FOR A MONTH.
I TOOK THE POST WHEN MY FATHER PASSED AWAY FROM ILLNESS.
I *NEED* IT, SO THAT I CAN SUCCEED MY FATHER'S PLACE AS HEAD OF HOUSE CAMPBELL.

DURING THE WAR DECADES AGO, THE GREAT MAN CALLED "HOUSMAN" BUILT THE BEGINNINGS OF WHAT WOULD BE THE INDEPENDENT TRADE CITY OF THAT SAME NAME.
HOUSMAN'S RIGHT-HAND MAN-- AND PERSONAL FRIEND-- WAS CAMPBELL. MY GRANDFATHER.
SINCE THEN, THE CAMPBELLS HAVE ALWAYS BEEN MEMBERS OF THE KNIGHT GUARD, DEDICATING THEIR LIVES TO THE PROTECTION OF THE CITY.
BUT TODAY, I GOT A HARSH LESSON.
GRIEVED AT THE TERRIBLE STATE OF THE CONTINENT, HE GAVE UP HIS RANK AS A NOBLE, AND DEVOTED HIS LIFE TO SECURING THE CITY'S INDEPENDENCE, AND SEEING IT FLOURISH.
PATHETICALLY WEAK. NOT JUST IN BODY, BUT IN MY HEART AND SOUL AS WELL.
SO I WANT ONE.
NO, I NEED ONE...
I KNOW NOW THAT I AM WEAK.

I NEED A "HEART" THAT CANNOT BREAK.
I NEED A BLADE THAT CAN PROTECT THE CITY, A BLADE THAT CAN UPHOLD MY HONOR. I NEED A BLADE THAT WILL BE MY PARTNER, MY OTHER HALF.
AND I WANT YOU, LUKE AINSWORTH, TO BE THE ONE TO FORGE THAT BLADE FOR ME!
ARE YOU FINISHED?
OR IS THERE MORE TO THIS SERMON?
IT'S NO SERMON. AS IT STANDS RIGHT NOW, IT IS NOTHING MORE THAN MY OWN SELFISH DESIRE.

THAT'S WHY I WANT YOU TO SEE ME!
HM?
WHAT?
HUH?
AH...!
"THAT'S WHY I WANT YOU TO SEE ME!"

STABBING
WHO COULD EVER FALL IN LOVE WITH THAT DRIED-UP, EMOTION-LESS STICK?!
THAT WAS UN-CALLED FOR...
I-I DIDN'T MEAN IT LIKE THAT!
N-NOT THAT!
OH MY~!
WOW... MISS CECILY, YOU'RE SO BOLD!
UH...
FIDGET FIDGET
ERM...
IT WAS NOT!!
A CON-FESSION OF LOVE...
POINT
I WOULD LIKE TO HIRE YOU AS A MERCENARY TO FIGHT ALONGSIDE MYSELF AND MY FELLOW KNIGHTS!
A-ANYWAY! TOMORROW, MY CORPS WILL LEAVE ON AN EXPEDITION.
HUFF HUFF
WE'RE GOING TO SUPPRESS BANDITS ON THE HIGH ROAD.
LUKE AINS-WORTH!
.....
?!

WATCH ME, LUKE AINSWORTH. JUDGE ME.
DETERMINE FOR YOURSELF IF I AM WORTHY OF CARRYING ONE OF YOUR BLADES.

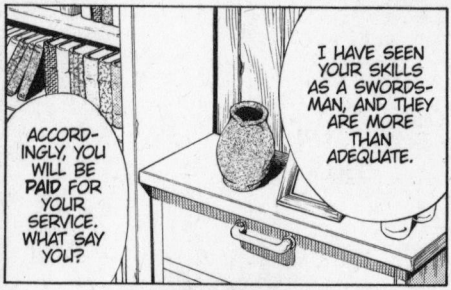
I HAVE SEEN YOUR SKILLS AS A SWORDSMAN, AND THEY ARE MORE THAN ADEQUATE.
ACCORDINGLY, YOU WILL BE PAID FOR YOUR SERVICE. WHAT SAY YOU?

ALL RIGHT.
!
REALLY?!
WHY NOT? IT SOUNDS LIKE IT MIGHT BE INTERESTING.

THE NEXT MORNING...
AAAAAH
LOKE
THIRD DISTRICT KNIGHT CORPS, MOVE OUT!
STOP SLOUCHING! HAVE A LITTLE MORE DIGNITY!
THEY'RE ALL WATCHING US!
TROMP
TROMP
STEP OUTSIDE HOUSMAN'S THIRD DISTRICT GATES...
WHY DID HE BRING THE GIRL?

AND YOU WILL BE GREETED WITH A WIDE VIEW OF FIELDS, ROLLING HILLS, AND THE PUBLIC HIGH ROAD, WHICH STRETCHES ALL THE WAY TO THE EMPIRE'S TERRITORY.
COME BACK HERE BIRDIE!
WE HAVE A BROAD AREA TO SEARCH, I'LL ADMIT. WE WILL TRY LOCATING THEIR BASE, FIRST.
HEY!
WHAT IS THE SIZE OF THE BANDIT MOB WE ARE LOOKING FOR?
OOH! A BIRDIE!
ACCORDING TO THOSE WHO'VE ESCAPED THEM, IT IS A GANG OF ABOUT TWENTY MEN.
SOME OF THE WITNESSES SAY THE GANG HAS SOME KIND OF INHUMAN BEAST TAMED AS A PET.
KYAA?!
OOPS, SHE TRIPPED
WE'VE HEARD SOME DISTURBING RUMORS.

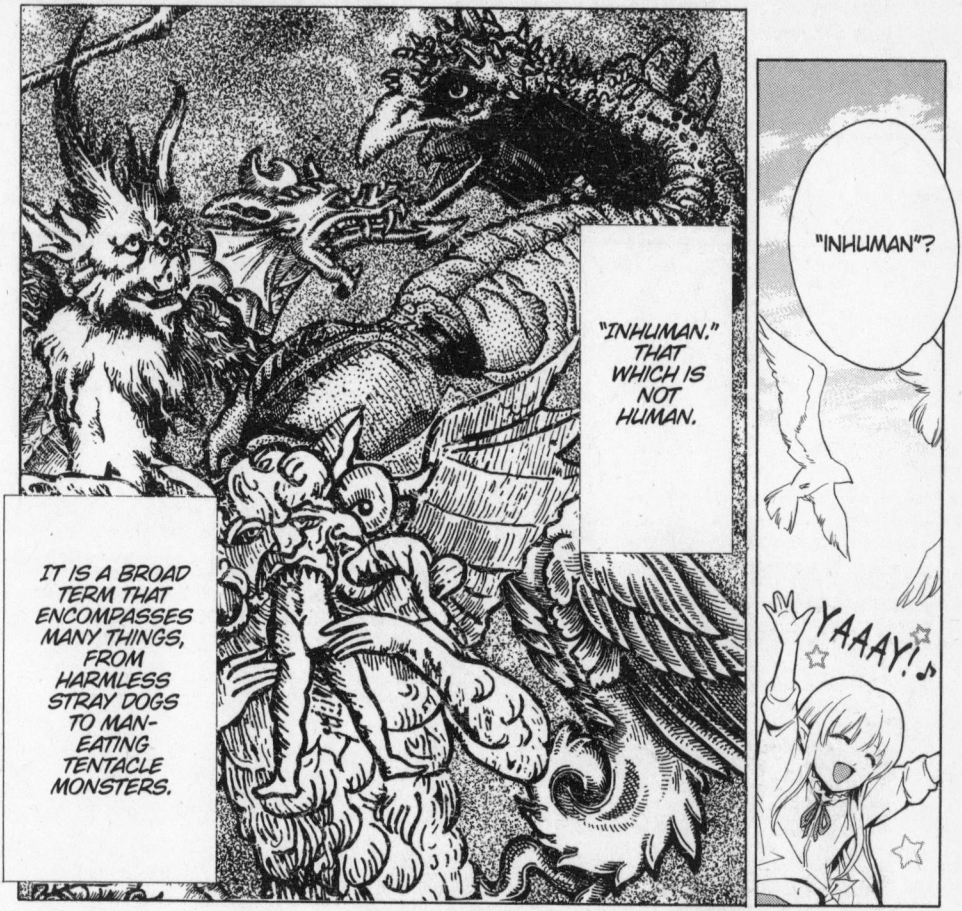
"INHUMAN." THAT WHICH IS NOT HUMAN.
IT IS A BROAD TERM THAT ENCOMPASSES MANY THINGS, FROM HARMLESS STRAY DOGS TO MAN-EATING TENTACLE MONSTERS.
"INHUMAN"?
YAAAY!♪

OH. ERM, YES. I DUG ONE OUT OF THE FAMILY'S STORE-HOUSE.
I SEE YOU HAVE A SWORD.

PLEASE WATCH OVER ME, FATHER. KEEP ME SAFE.
BUT I KEPT THE FIRST ONE.
IT MAY BE BROKEN, BUT IT IS STILL A SYMBOL OF HOUSE CAMPBELL'S HONOR.
IT DOESN'T.
I AM A BLACKSMITH AFTER ALL.
!
I-I KNOW IT MAY SEEM CHILDISH, BUT, UM...
I DON'T DISLIKE THOSE WHO RESPECT THEIR BLADES.

LUKE...

D-DON'T GO SAYING THINGS LIKE THAT OUT IN PUBLIC!
IT'S EMBAR-RASS-ING!
STAP STAP STAP STAP
WHAT DID YOU THINK I WAS SAYING? GODS!

IF YOU DON'T MIND ME ASKING, WHAT IS LISA TO YOU?
MY LIVE-IN ASSISTANT.
REALLY. NOW, I VERY MUCH HOPE THIS ISN'T TRUE, LUKE AINSWORTH, BUT...
YOU DON'T HAVE THOSE TASTES, DO YOU?

IT SEEMS THAT AT SOME POINT, I AM GOING TO NEED TO HAVE A VERY SERIOUS DISCUSSION WITH YOU...
AND I, WITH YOU.
I... FOUND HER.
MISS CECILY!

I KNOW WHERE THE BANDITS LIVE!
THESE LITTLE BIRDIES TOLD ME.
HUH ?!
IT'S THIS WAY! ♪
HEY!
W-WAIT!
WHA ?
?!
I THOUGHT IT MIGHT BE USEFUL. SO I BROUGHT HER ALONG.
OH, DID I FORGET TO MENTION? LISA CAN SPEAK WITH ANIMALS.
THANKS, BIRDIES!
I DON'T THINK "CONVENIENCE" IS THE ISSUE HERE!

WELL...
WE FOUND THEM. VERY... ABRUPTLY.

WHILE THIS SCENE IS, ADMITTEDLY, JUST AN UNHAPPY ACCIDENT...
WHIZZZ
GRRRRR!!
I'LL CUT IT TO PIECES !!
RMBL RMBL RMBL RMBL
THE SHEER EMBARRASSMENT OF SEEING SOMETHING A YOUNG LADY DOESN'T WANT TO SEE IS MOST DEFINITELY STILL THERE.
AND IT TRIGGERED AN EXPLOSION OF RAGE THAT BUBBLED UP, RIGHT OUT OF MY SOUL.
EVERY MAN IN THE AREA IMMEDIATELY CLENCHED HIS KNEES TOGETHER.

TROMP
TROMP
TROMP
TROMP
AAAH!!
COME BACK HERE, YOU THIEVES!!
LUKE!
WATCH NOW. WATCH ME CAREFULLY!
FWEEEEE
FLMP
FLMP
FLMP
FLMP
DAMMIT!
HN.

GAH!
THUK
ZWISH
HUNH ?!
LOOK OUT!
THEY'RE SHOOTING AT US FROM THE TREES!!
WHERE ?!
THNK
OW ...!
DAMMIT!
WHEEEM
AND WHAT IS A PRAYER PACT, YOU ASK...?
A PRAYER PACT!
RIGHT !
EVERYONE, GET DOWN! I'M GOING TO USE A PRAYER PACT!

FWOOSH
VWEEE
MAGES CAN AGITATE SPIRITS IN THE AIR, CAUSING A REACTION.
THIS REACTION CAN BE THINGS LIKE, SAY, A WHIRLWIND.
USING A CHUNK OF SMELTED IRON SAND, CALLED "JEWEL STEEL," AS A MEDIUM...
FRUUU
BWOOOOSH
ALL IN ALL, IT IS A VERY CONVENIENT THING TO HAVE HANDY!

GAH!
FWOOOO
SHRING
WAAAAAAH?!
THUMP
THERE HE IS!

POINT
URK!
FREEZE!
MOVE AND YOU WILL BE STRUCK DOWN!

WE ARE THE KNIGHT GUARD, TASKED WITH SECURING THE SAFETY OF THESE ROADS.
SEVERAL MERCHANT CARAVANS CARRYING GOODS BETWEEN THE EMPIRE AND THE INDEPENDENT TRADE CITIES HAVE REPORTED BEING ATTACKED BY BANDITS IN THIS AREA.
THOSE BANDITS ARE YOU, CORRECT?

WHAT'S SO FUNNY?!
ANSWER THE QUESTION, OR--
WHERE ARE THE REST OF YOU?
TALK, THIEF!
HEH HEH.
AWOOOOO
?!

WOOOO

AW
AW
AWOOOOO

.....
WH-WHAT WAS THAT?

LUKE.

SOME KIND OF BEAST'S HOWL...?

NO...
THAT RUMOR! THE ONE WHICH SAID THEY HAD TAMED AN INHUMAN BEAST...
YAGH!
HEY!
SCAMPER
COME BACK HERE, YOU SCUM!!
AFTER HIM! DON'T LET HIM ESCAPE!!
STMP
STMP
STMP
STMP
WAIT ...!
SKSH
SKSH
SKSH
SKSH
SKSH

OO
FWOOSH

AWOOOO

INHUMANS --!!
WHUCK
SPLUCH
GODS--! THE BANDITS REALLY DID HAVE THEM!
DAMMIT!!
TMP
TMP
TMP
TMP
TMP
TMP

SLASH
SPLISH
SPLAT.

THUK
WHUNK
SPLAK
HURRR
AH...
AAAAA-AHHHH!!
SWIPE
SWIP
SWIP

OOF !!
NGH ...
KOFF...
WH-WHA...
WHAT'S HAPPENING ...?

I HAVEN'T DONE ANYTHING YET.
I HAVEN'T PROTECTED ANYONE...
W-WAIT...
.....
GLENGH
IS IT ALL GOING TO END BEFORE I CAN EVEN BEGIN?!

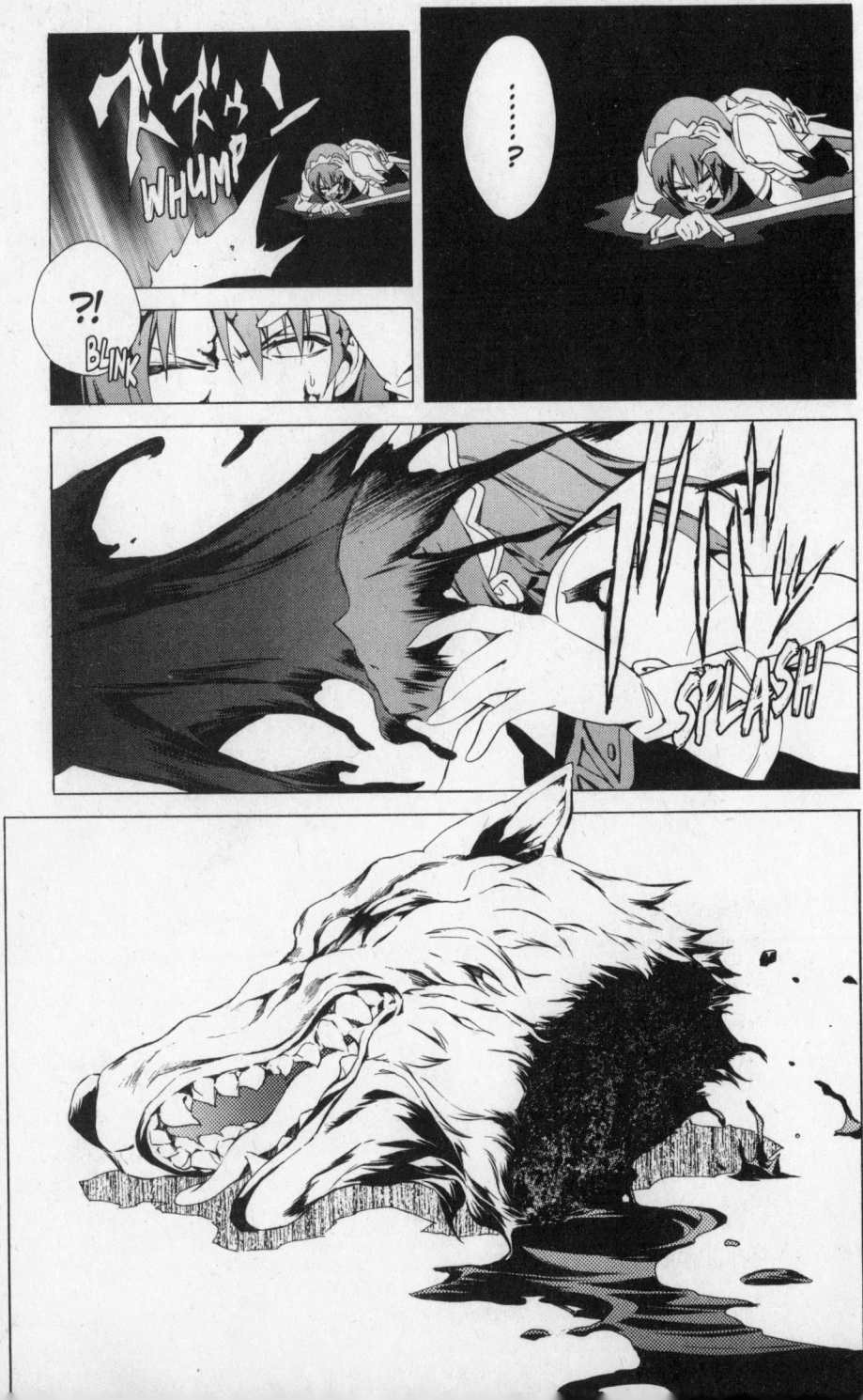
……?
ズズゥ
WHUMP
?!
BLINK
SPLASH

STAND, CECILY CAMPBELL.

WHUMP
OR ARE YOU ALL BARK AND NO BITE?
.....!
HERE COME THE REST OF THEM.
RSSSTL...

LISA.
HERE, LUKE.
SHF
WIPE
WIPE
TOSS
DON'T LITTER!
YOU THERE...
BANDITS. DON'T THINK OF RUNNING AWAY NOW.
URK...

YGRAAAAAH
CLENCH
DON'T WORRY, MISS CECILY. EVERYTHING'LL BE OKAY NOW.
LUKE HAS FINALLY DECIDED TO GET SERIOUS!
WHOOSH
GLEAM

SLGE
RG
A
A
A
A
H!!
GY
OW
R!!
SKSHH

SLIK

SPLURCH

WISH

YOOOWL
SLICE
TOO SHALLOW!
SHING
WHRL

FWOOSH
SPLURT

HE'S INCREDIBLE!
THE SHARPNESS OF THAT KATANA IS A THING OF WONDER, BUT THOSE SKILLS...!
GODS...
STANDARD SWORDSMANSHIP HERE INVOLVES HAVING A SHIELD ON THE LEFT ARM.
THUS THE BASIC STANCE IS A THREE-QUARTER POSITION, WITH THE LEFT SIDE FORWARD AND THE RIGHT SIDE BACK.
BUT HIS IS THE REVERSE!
HE DOES NOT STEP FORWARD WITH HIS LEFT FOOT...

AND HIS STRIKES ARE GRACEFUL AND POWERFUL, USING HIS ENTIRE BODY.
IT'S ALMOST AS IF HE DOESN'T PICK UP HIS FEET AT ALL.
LUKE AINSWORTH...
JUST WHO ARE YOU...?
!
HAAH ...
HAAH ...

HE IS.
LUKE ALWAYS HAS TO DODGE THE ENEMY'S STRIKES BY A HAIR'S BREADTH.

STRANGE... IT ALMOST LOOKS AS IF HE IS STARTING TO HAVE TROUBLE.

DO YOU SEE WHERE I'M GOING?

SO JOINING COMBAT WITHOUT ANY WAY TO STOP A BLADE IS JUST PLAIN UNTHINKABLE.
TO LOSE YOUR WEAPON ON THE BATTLEFIELD MEANS DEATH, RIGHT?

WHAT KIND OF BLADE IS THAT KATANA, ANYWAY?

EVEN LUKE'S KATANA.
ALL BLADES GET DULLED, AND EVEN BREAK WHEN YOU USE THEM.
IT MEANS HE DOESN'T HAVE A CHOICE BUT TO KEEP COMING WITHIN A HAIR'S BREADTH OF DEATH, IN RAPID SUCCESSION!

KATANAS ARE MADE BY ONLY A FEW BLACKSMITHS, THOSE WHO HAVE FOUND AN OLD, OLD WAY OF FORGING BLADES.
IT'S CALLED "FOLDED STEEL." BLACKSMITHS WORK FOR HOURS, DILIGENTLY FOLDING AND TEMPERING THE METAL REPEATEDLY.
THE RESULTING BLADE IS CALLED A "KATANA."
SWORDS MASS-PRODUCED FROM MOLDS DON'T EVEN COME CLOSE TO IT, IN TERMS OF STURDINESS AND SHARPNESS.
.....!
HIS STYLE OF "VICTORY THROUGH INITIATIVE"... IS THAT A RESULT OF THE BLADE'S SPECIAL ATTRIBUTES?
ANY-WAY...
LUKE SHOULD BE ABLE TO CLEAN UP ALL THIS BY HIMSELF JUST FINE...

BATHMP
BUT ARE YOU SURE YOU'RE OKAY WITH THAT?

"I WANT YOU TO SEE ME!"
NO.
CLENCH
"I WANT YOU TO SEE ME!"
NO, IT'S NOT!!
NOT THIS ME...
BECAUSE THIS ME...

BOOOM!
!
I MUST NEVER ACCEPT !!
HAAH !!
SWASH

THE FEELING OF BLADE IMPACTING FLESH, SHUDDERING UP SWORD TO ARM, THEN ARM TO SHOULDER.
THAT SUDDEN, RAW JOLT.
WHUK
KLANG
LET THE RAGE OUT!
DON'T HESI-TATE.
SKSHHHH

SO I HAVE TO MAKE UP FOR WHAT I LACK IN TECHNIQUE WITH SHEER EMOTION!
HIS STYLE WILL NEVER BE MINE.
I CAN'T BE LIKE LUKE...
HYAAAAAH!!!
SHOVE

N-
NO
WAY...!
SPLAK
NEXT
!!

YOU HAVEN'T WON YET, WENCH!!
GAK?!
!!
SLASH
QUIT WASTING TIME ON WORDS!
!
YOU'RE A MORE PASSIONATE WOMAN THAN I HAD THOUGHT, THOUGH YOU SEEM TO HAVE MISPLACED YOUR FEMININE RESTRAINT.
INTERESTING, CECILY CAMPBELL.

But these demons were not summoned from the depths of hell. They were made through the sacrifice of human flesh.

The Valbanill War

—Valbanill—

That sentime stems fr one sing thing the Dem Pacts.

Their use meant that men did not fight other men, instead, they fought demons and hell-beasts. Thus it was named "The Valbanill War."

The Sacred Blacksmith

聖剣の刀鍛冶（ブラックスミス）

Cecily Campbell

IT WILL BE ALL RIGHT.
WE CAN DO THIS.
I CAN DO THIS !!

BUT THAT ONE FIGHT TAUGHT US ALL SOMETHING WE NEVER EXPECTED.
AND THE BATTLE CAME TO A SWIFT CLOSE.
THE BANDITS WERE QUICKLY ROUNDED UP...

WE LEARNED ABOUT THE TERROR THAT A DEMON PACT COULD BRING...

WHAT ARE ALL OF YOU WAITING FOR?!
STAND! DO YOUR DUTY, AND BRING JUSTICE !!
R-RIGHT!
LET'S GET THEM !!

Thus the one thing that nearly drove the entire continent to ruin was safely consigned to oblivion. Or so everyone thought...

When the war finally ended, every kingdom unanimously agreed to ban the use of Demon Pacts.

Chapter 2 Knight (Part 2)

GURK!
SLASH
STAND AND FIGHT, KNIGHTS!
RMBL
RMBL
RMBL
RMBL
RMBL
DO NOT LET A SINGLE BANDIT GET AWAY!!

AAAH !!
CECILY CAMPBELL! COME WITH ME.
HURRY! THE LAST ONE IS ESCAPING !
LUKE! LISA!
RSTL
RSTL
RSTL
RSTL
WSH
HUFF ...
HUFF ...

GIVE UP! YOU CAN'T ESCAPE US.
WE ARE GOING TO HAVE A LONG TALK, BECAUSE I DOUBT ANY ORDINARY BANDIT GANG COULD KEEP INHUMANS AS PETS.
HOLD! SOME-THING IS WRONG.
HUH?
WHAT IS HE DOING?
HEH HEH ...
HEH HEH HEH.
SKCH

LUKE ...?
LISA?
.....
BTHMP
BTHMP
WHAT ?!

CECILY CAMPBELL, GET BACK! NOW!!
WHAT? WHY?!
THAT WAS A "DEATH PHRASE" !!
DOOM

A DEATH PHRASE ...?!
BUT YOU CAN'T MEAN... THAT DEATH PHRASE ...!
TWITCH
SHUDDER
TWITCH
SHUDDER
TWITCH
TWITCH
YES. THE TRIGGER FOR A DEMON PACT!
SHUDDER
SHUDDER
TWITCH
SHUDDER
SHUDDER
TWITCH
TWITCH

POK
GAAAAH!!

DON'T LOOK AWAY.
.....
AAAA

SPLOK
GYAARGH !!!
OH ...
OH MY GODS ...!
SPLOK
THE OFFERING OF FLESH, AND THE FORGING OF A DEMON PACT.
I AM SURE YOU HAVE AT LEAST HEARD OF THIS.

SPOOK
SPOOK
BUT THIS MAN... HE GOT DESPERATE AND TOSSED ALL CARE TO THE WINDS!
AMATEURS LIKE HIM IRRITATE ME TO NO END!

TYPICALLY, THOSE WHO HAVE MADE A DEMON PACT ARE LIKE THE VAGRANT FROM THE OTHER DAY. THEY OFFER ONLY A SMALL PIECE OF THEMSELVES.

LIKE IN THE WAR?!

OPEN YOUR EYES TO REALITY !!

SPOOK
SPOOK
SPOOK
W-WAIT ...
H-HE CAN'T BE MAKING A DEMON PACT. THOSE WERE FORBIDDEN BY THE WHOLE CONTI--

YIKES. HAS THAT BANDIT REALLY MADE LIKE THIS ANGRY...?

FOOOM
?!

SWOOOO

!
SWOOO

WHAT JUST HAPPENED ...?

KA-SHONK
カシャ
カシャ
SHONK

NO, IT'S DIFFERENT. YE GODS, WHAT IS THAT THING?
AN ICE BEAST ?!
IT HAS THE SHAPE OF A BEAST, BUT THERE'S NO LIVING WARMTH TO IT AT ALL!

FWOOO
KREK
KREK
KREK
KREK
KREK
KREK
KREK
KREK
KREK
DON'T JUST STAND THERE STARING! MOVE BEFORE...
FSHOOOM

THUK
GURK ...!

!!
NNH ...
THOOM
THOOM

SHOOSH
PTANG

GYA HA HA HA HA HA
KLANG
AH HA HA HA HA
WSH
YES, SIR!
LISA?
I HAVE NO CHOICE.
RST
TCH.
THMP

IT'S BEEN AGES, BUT IT LOOKS LIKE IT'S TIME TO DO *THAT* AGAIN.

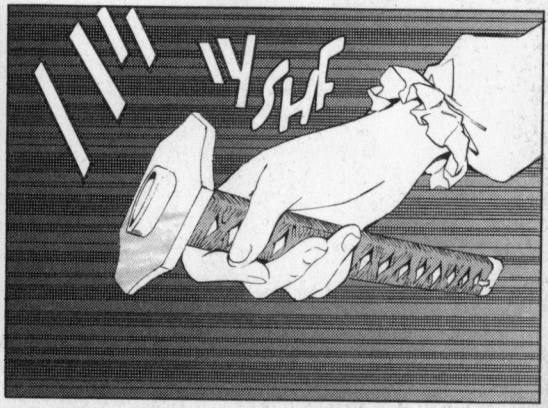
SHF

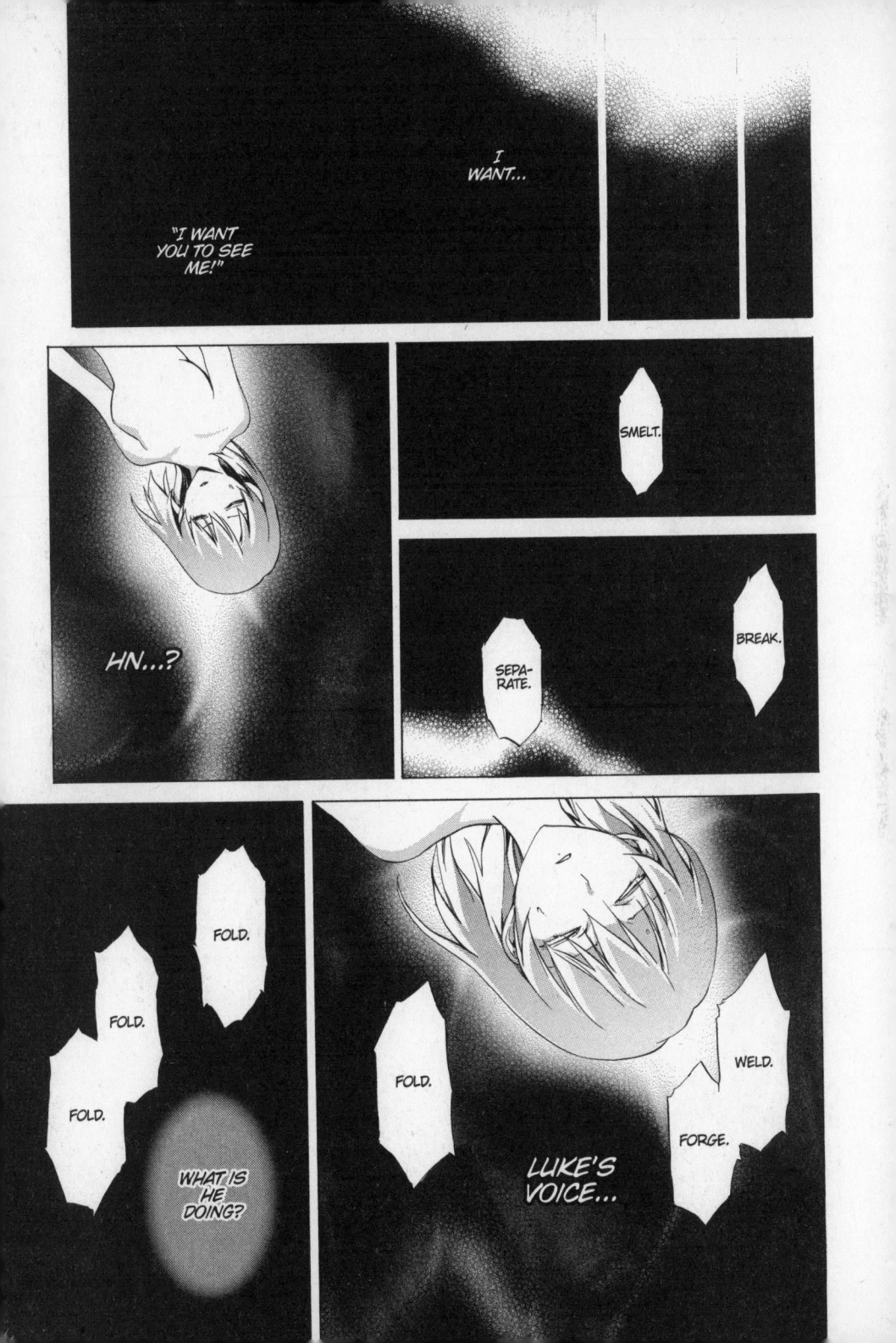
I WANT...
"I WANT YOU TO SEE ME!"
SMELT.
HN...?
BREAK.
SEPA-RATE.
FOLD.
FOLD.
FOLD.
WHAT IS HE DOING?
WELD.
FOLD.
FORGE.
LUKE'S VOICE...

FOLD.
FOLD.
.....
CORE STEEL, COMPLETE. SKIN STEEL, COMPLETE.
?!

CLAY COAT, ROUGH FINISH.
BLADE CON-STRUC-TION: FINAL STAGE.
HEAT.
CUT POINT.
BLADE CON-STRUC-TION: DRAW.
WHAT DO YOU THINK YOU'RE DOING, AT A TIME LIKE THIS?!
LIKE, LISA...
THUM
THUM
THUM
THUM
THUM
THUM
OH, CRAP!
STRAIGHT-EN.
THE BEAST IS MOVING TO ATTACK AGAIN!
SHARP-EN.

FSHOOOM
FOUN-DATION POLISH: BINSUI STONE.
KAISEI STONE.
TCH!
IT WON'T BE FINISHED IN TIME!
CHU-NAGURA STONE.
KOMA-NAGURA STONE.
DAMMIT, WHO CARES WHAT THEY'RE DOING!
IT IS MY DUTY TO PROTECT THE CITIZENS OF THE CITY!!
I AM THE CURRENT MASTER OF THE HONORABLE AND VENERABLE HOUSE CAMPBELL!
CHING

WHAT ARE YOU--
?!
BLOCK!
LUKE!
WATCH ME...!

THIS IS WHO I, CECILY CAMPBELL, REALLY AM!!
UCHIGO-MORI STONE.
FINAL POLISH: JIZUYA STONE.
NUGUI.
HADORI FINISH. MIRROR POLISH. TIP POLISH.

KA-CHING
MOUNT HILT.

FWMP

THANKS TO YOU, I WAS ABLE TO COMPLETE IT, UNINTER-RUPTED.

LUKE...

BWOOOOSH
NOW, LEAVE THE REST OF THIS TO ME!

Luke Ainsworth

The Sacred Blacksmith

聖剣の刀鍛冶（ブラックスミス）

A RED KATANA!!
BWOOSH
BUT, WHERE DID HE GET IT? AND WHY IS IT RED? IS IT BURNING, MAYBE?
NO, NEVER MIND ANY OF THAT RIGHT NOW...
GO FOR IT, LUKE!

Chapter 3
Knight
(Part 3)

SHOOSH
CLANG
SLICE

GYA AAA AA RR!!
INCRED-IBLE! IT BURNED ITS WAY CLEAN THROUGH THE ICE BEAST'S HIDE!!
FWOOM
SWOOM
AH--! LOOK OUT!!
FWSH

FWOOO
THM
THM
THM
THM
THM
KRM
KRM
LUKE ...?
KRM
KRM
KRM

THUNK!!
LUKE !!
KRASH

SLASH

SWOOOSH
WSH

KRAK
CRASH

SNAP
TINK
TINK
TINK

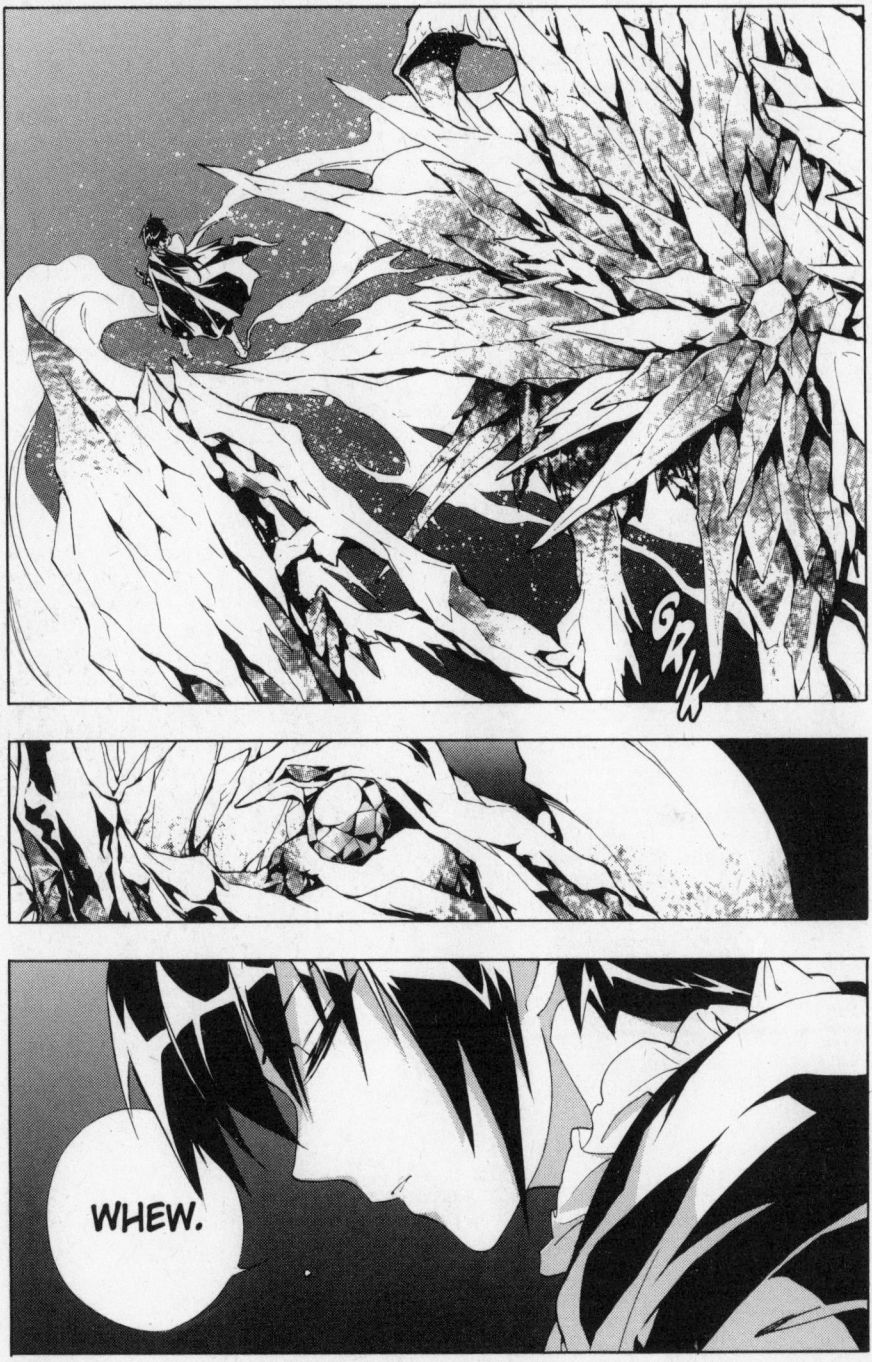
GRIK
WHEW.

FWSHHH

HUH? LISA...?

HE DID IT!

PSHUU
UM! Y-YOU LOOKED AWFULLY DIZZY THERE, MISS CECILY!
SO, UM...
I... I WAS JUST HELPING YOU STAY STANDING BY HOLDING ON TO YOU! FR-FROM BEHIND!
HEE HEE HEE!
IT'S OKAY, LISA. THE MONSTER IS GONE. LUKE KILLED IT.
IT IS...?
STAGGER
ARE YOU OKAY?! THAT BEAST DIDN'T GET YOU, DID IT?!!
OH MY GOSH! LUKE!
YOU'RE BLEEDING!!
!
HA HA HA!
AHA HA HA!
URK!
SPLRT

I...I'M FINE. JUST DO SOMETHING ABOUT... ABOUT THAT!
JIGGLE
"THAT" ...?

@MC☆※▲!!
KA-POW!
WHHD
GYAH!!
WHA...
WHY ME?!
BIFF!
POW
SOK!
WHAK!
!!
AAAHHH!!!
AAAAAAHH!!

A BANDIT GANG WHO USED INHUMANS, AND CREATED DEMON PACTS...
THERE HAS TO BE SOMETHING MORE THERE.
I MUST REPORT THIS TO THE CAPTAIN, AS SOON AS I RETURN.
PLANS NEED TO BE DEVISED IMMEDIATELY!
TMP TMP
GLANCE
ERM... I APOLOGIZE. I...I WAS DISTRESSED.
AH... UM...
DO YOU ALWAYS BEAT THE MOST CONVENIENT PERSON TO A PULP WHEN YOU GET "DISTRESSED"?
DON'T GET MAD, LUKE...
I MEAN, YOU WERE THE ONE WHO GOT A NOSE BLEED FROM JUST A LITTLE PEEK.
HAPPPH
HEE HEE! WHO WOULD'VE GUESSED YOU WERE SUCH AN INNOCENT!
SHUT UP, OR I'M KICKING YOU OUT.
THEY WERE SO BIG AND BOUNCY, TOO!
I WISH MINE WERE THAT BIG!
CAN WE DROP THIS SUBJECT NOW?!

BY THE WAY...
LUKE AINSWORTH.

HAVE YOU THOUGHT OVER THE REQUEST I MADE YESTERDAY?

HE ONLY HAS ONE EYE.
THAT ONE, HIS LEFT, IS FLAT AND LIFELESS.

NO... HE IS A MYSTERY, BUT I MUSTN'T PRY. THAT WOULD BE BOORISH.
THEN THERE WAS THAT DARK BALL OF FLAME, AND THE KATANA HE DREW FROM IT.
HE SAID HE HAD GIVEN UP THE ART OF FORGING SWORDS, BUT HE WIELDS ONE WELL. VERY WELL.
WHO ARE YOU, LUKE...?
AND HE IS FAMILIAR WITH DEMON PACTS.
AND ALL I NEED FROM HIM IS JUST ONE THING ALONE!
WILL YOU FORGE A BLADE FOR ME?

SKFF
SKFF

SKFF

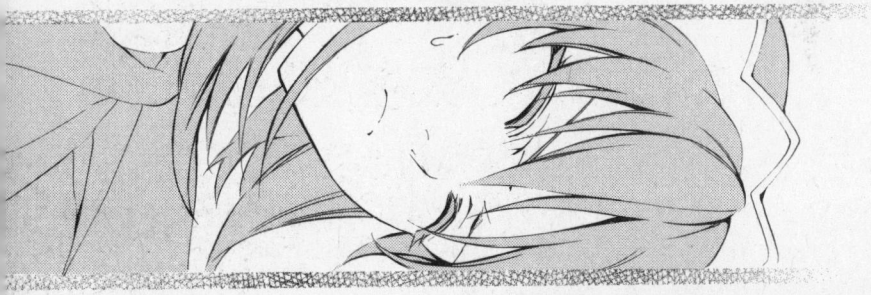

PAT

LUKE... THANK YOU!
ALL RIGHT.
AH!
ぐいっ

I PROMISE YOU, LUKE...

THAT BLADE WILL ONLY EVER BE USED IN THE DEFENSE OF THE CITY AND ITS PEOPLE.
FOR THAT REASON...
AS IT IS FOR EVERYONE'S SAKE...
PLEASE MAKE ME...
PLEASE! MAKE ME THE GREATEST SWORD IN THE WORLD!!

HM? WHAT IS IT?
.....
NOTHING.
I JUST... HEARD SOMETHING SIMILAR FROM SOMEONE ELSE, A LONG TIME AGO.
THEY ARE SO ALIKE.
IT'S NOTHING... FORGET IT.

I USE ONLY THE HIGHEST QUALITY OF JEWEL STEEL IN MY CREATIONS, WHICH MEANS THEY ARE MUCH, MUCH MORE EXPENSIVE THAN THE JUNK YOU FIND AROUND HERE.
LUM, LUKE ...?
WHAT DO YOU MEAN, "HUH?"
YOU CANNOT SERIOUSLY THINK I WILL FORGE YOU A SWORD SIMPLY OUT OF THE GOODNESS OF MY HEART.
WELL, AREN'T YOU NAIVE.
NOW, LET US TALK ABOUT MY PAYMENT.
HUH?
GOOONG
UP FRONT.
HELL NO.
LUMP-SUM PAYMENT AFTER DELIVERY ...?
LUM... IS IT POSSIBLE TO SET UP A PAYMENT PLAN?
NOT MY PROBLEM.
ERM... MY WAGES ARE, UH, NOT EXACTLY ALL THAT HIGH...
TMP TMP
YOU... YOU SKINFLINT! MISER! YOU PENNY-PINCHER !!
.....

AND SO IT SEEMS IT WILL BE QUITE SOME TIME YET BEFORE CECILY CAMPBELL GETS HER NEW SWORD.

YAMMER?
ガヤ
BUSTLE
ワイ
BUSTLE
ワイ
ガヤ
YAMMER?
A MARKET, EH...?

AHA HA HA HA!
YSEE...
OH... RIGHT.
THAT FESTIVAL IS COMING SOON.

GODS TAKE IT ALL...
WHERE IS MY SALVATION ...?
THINGS THAT ONLY STRANGERS IN A FARAWAY LAND GET TO ENJOY.
FESTIVALS. DRINKING.
FEASTING...
?
NO, THEY WERE NO GOOD AT ALL.
HEE HEE! YES, THIS SORT OF THING IS BEST LEFT TO THOSE WITH EXPERIENCE.
BEGINNERS ARE NO GOOD.
PARDON ME.
NO, THEY DID NOT DO WELL AT ALL. THAT IS WHY, THIS TIME, I WILL DO YOU THE FAVOR.
NOT ONLY DID THEY RUN WILD-- SO STUPID!-- BUT THEY DID IT WHERE THEY WERE QUICKLY FOUND. SO FOOLISH! AND WORSE YET, THEY WERE CAUGHT TOO SOON.

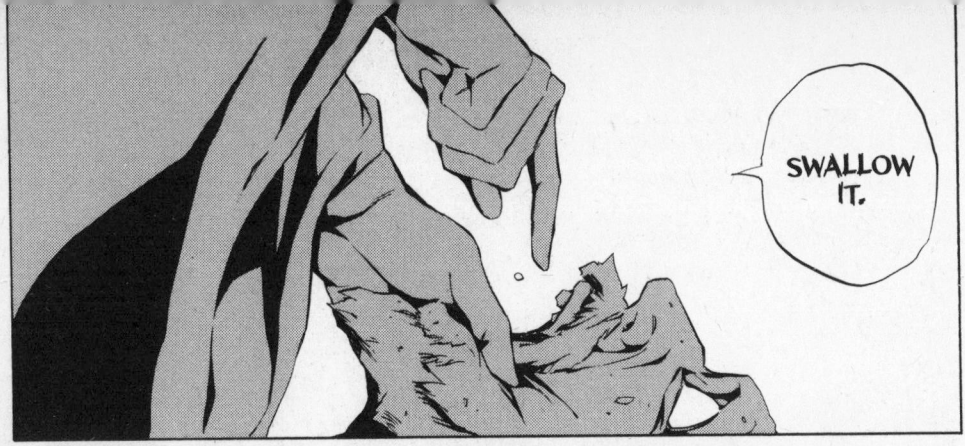
SWALLOW IT.

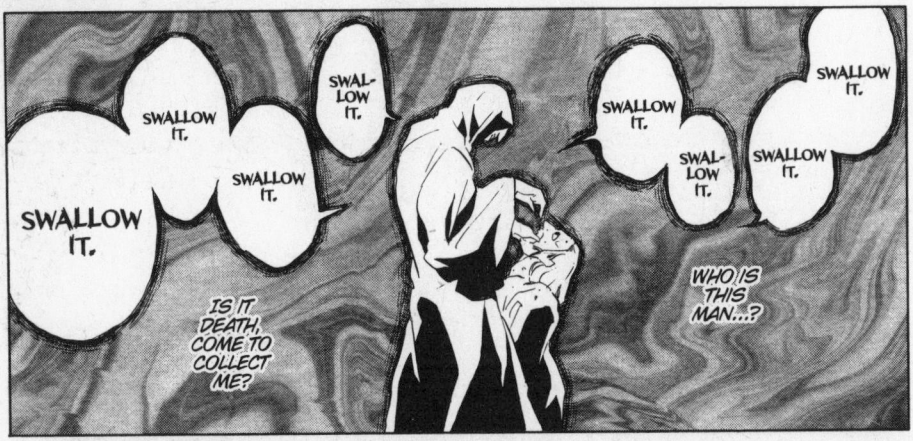
SWALLOW IT.
SWALLOW IT.
SWALLOW IT.
SWAL-LOW IT.
IS IT DEATH, COME TO COLLECT ME?
SWALLOW IT.
SWAL-LOW IT.
SWALLOW IT.
SWALLOW IT.
WHO IS THIS MAN...?

NO, NOT DEATH...

SWALLOW IT AAALL DOWN!!
THERE YOU GO...

HE IS A DEMON!
YOU WANTED TO SPEAK WITH ME, COMMANDER?
YES. WELL DONE ON YOUR EXPEDITION THE OTHER DAY.
HOW-EVER...
I HAVE BAD NEWS ABOUT THE BANDITS YOU HAD CAPTURED.
THIRD DISTRICT KNIGHT GUARD CAPTAIN —HANNIBAL QUASAR—

WHAT ?!
I WILL BE BLUNT. ALL SEVENTEEN OF THEM WERE KILLED IN THEIR CELLS LAST NIGHT.
IT WAS A BLOODY SCENE.
THEY OBVIOUSLY SUFFERED, BLEEDING FROM EVERY ORIFICE THEY HAD.
GOODS THAT WILL BE PUT UP FOR AUCTION AT THIS YEAR'S MARKET.
!
HOWEVER, WE ARE NOT LEFT ENTIRELY IN THE LURCH. WE DID MANAGE TO DISCOVER WHAT THE BANDITS WERE AFTER.
GODS...!
IT WAS NO NATURAL DEATH. ONLY A SPECIFIC PARASITE CAN KILL A MAN SO. THOSE BANDITS WERE VERY DELIBERATELY SILENCED.

AUCTION GOODS...?
ANYTHING IN PARTICULAR?
YES, THE DEMON BLADE ARIA.
To be continued...

✳ *Lisa* ✳

The Sacred Blacksmith

聖剣の刀鍛治（ブラックスミス）

Lisa's Let's Learn Blacksmithing Corner!

Thank you so much for reading *The Sacred Blacksmith!* I'm Lisa, the assistant at Atelier Liza. ♪
How was Volume 1? With this corner, I hope to show you lots more things that will help you to enjoy the world of *The Sacred Blacksmith* even more! So without further ado, come on in!

Class #1: Making A Katana ~Part 1~

Why is Luke's sword so amazing?!

It never bends, it never breaks, and it's extremely sharp!

Unlike the straight swords that knights like Cecily use, Luke's katana has a distinctive curve. It may have broken during his fight with the demon in Chapter 2, but a knight with a normal sword wouldn't have been able to fight at all! A katana is a very powerful blade, strong enough to even cut into axes, like in Chapter 1. But what makes it that strong?

Sharp-eyed readers will have noticed that Luke's katana is modeled on the real-world Japanese katana. Unlike most swords, Japanese katana are made of two different types of steel, giving it the toughness to stay sharp, and the resilience to avoid breaking. But that's not much of an explanation. What exactly goes into making a Japanese katana?

Even Miss Cecily wanted a sword like Luke's. But how do people make blades that are so incredible? Turn to the next page, where I explain all about how they're made! ♪

How To Forge A Japanese Katana

It doesn't break! It doesn't bend! It's super sharp!

Are just a few words not enough? Here's a detailed explanation of the forging process! ☆

The 3-Step Forging Process

1. Assemble the correct steels.
2. Forge the steels.
3. Shape the blade.

1 Smelting & Separation

Katanas are made from a special metal called "jewel steel." But jewel steel comes in awkward, lumpy "blooms," so they need to be melded together (smelting), and then cut into easy-to-use pieces (separation).

2 Welding & Forging

Next, the pieces of jewel steel are covered in clay, stacked in a pile, and heated in the furnace. When the clay melts off, they're pulled out as one single lump. The blacksmith will then hammer the lump into a block about 6 x 9cm in size.

3 Folding

Now that we have the materials, it's time to forge the blade! The jewel steel block is heated in the furnace and then drawn into a long bar. The bar is folded back on itself, reheated, and drawn out into a long bar again. This is repeated about 15 times. Man, does it take a lot of strength! This process evens out the carbon content and pounds any impurities out of the steel.

Building the Skin Steel

The result of the folding process is a hard steel known as "skin steel." Katanas are made from this steel, and the softer steel that the skin steel wraps around is called "core steel." Both types of steel are made at the same time.

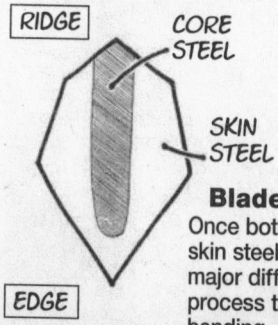

Building the Core Steel

Core steel is a softer metal made from iron mixed with a little jewel steel. They are heated and folded together in a process just like that for skin steel.

Blade Construction

Once both steels are ready, it's time to wrap the hard, carbon-rich skin steel around the soft, carbon-poor core steel. This is the first major difference between the katana and other swords. It's this process that gives the katana the hardness that keeps it from bending, and the flexibility that prevents it from breaking.

The weight of the steel determines how long the blade will be, so blacksmiths hammer away to draw the blade out to just the right length!

4 Elongation

Now that the two types of steel are put together, the result is heated and carefully drawn out into a "blank," the basic shape of the sword. Blacksmiths keep the final shape they want the blade to be firmly in mind during this step.

5 Cutting the Point

Once the blank is finished, the blacksmith goes chop-chop, and cuts the end off on the diagonal. The tip is then heated in the forge and shaped from the edge back to the ridge into its distinct curve.

6 Shaping the Blade

Once the blank is made and the tip is cut, the general shape of the blade is finished. Next, on to some refinements! The blade is once again heated in the forge, and the edge is made. A rasp is used to even out the thickness. Next up, refining the blade's distinctive curve and the hamon temper line.

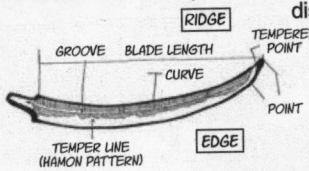

7 Rough Finish

The surface of the blade is cleaned with a very rough type of whetstone, called an "arato." A big plane that can hone even pig steel, the arato will grind down all the little dips and bumps until the blade is perfectly smooth!

8 Clay Coat

Heat-resistant clay is mixed with charcoal powder and polishing stone powder to make "blade clay." This determines the pattern of the blade's "hamon" or temper line, so the blade clay is applied very carefully in waves. The part of the blade that needs the most heat only gets a thin coat. The rest of the blade is coated thickly.

9 Finishing the Blade

Once the blade clay has dried on the blade, it is heated in the furnace to about 8,000 degrees! The blacksmith will then pull it out at the right moment, and quench it in a barrel of water. That's what makes the blade curve! Blacksmiths know the exact moment to pull the blade out by its color, but figuring out what that "right color" is takes practice.

Depending on how the blacksmith puts on the blade clay, the curve of the blade will change. The thinly-covered edge will get really hard, and the thickly-covered ridge will become much more supple! When cooled, it gives the katana its distinctive curve.

The main storyline mentions the names of many of these stages, but now you have a better idea of what they really involve! This isn't the end, though. There's lots and lots more steps to go! So next time, we'll talk about the "polishing" stages that finish the blade. Hope you're looking forward to it as much as I am!

There are many more steps after this, including straightening the blade, setting the edge, polishing, and many other important things. Once all of those are done, the Japanese katana is finally complete!

To Be Continued!

"Whoa, this is more fun than the original novels!"

That was the first thing that popped into my head when I read the first chapter of the manga. "Oh crap," I remember thinking. "I could be in trouble here."

I never dreamed the manga would be able to expand the world so much, or bring it to such vibrant life. I await each new chapter with both trepidation and breathless anticipation.

Yamada-sensei, thank you. Thank you, thank you, thank you. I look forward to more of your awesome and awe-inspiring work. Luna-san and I won't let ourselves fall short of your standard!

–Novel Author
Isao Miura

Miura Isao

Congratulations on the publishing of Volume 1!
Yamada-san, I can't wait to see more of your Miss Cecily and Friends in action!

A Lazy Afterword

Baseball Fan NAKAMURA-SAN

Tetris Master YAMADA-SAN

Lover of Rice YOSHINO-SAN

SEPA-
RATE.
SMELT.
BREAK.
WELD.
The Sacred Blacksmith: PREVIEW
FWOOOO
FOLD.
FOLD.
FWOOO
FORGE.

FWOOOOOO
FOLD.
FOLD.
FOLD.

I HEARD THIS WAS A SMITHY.
I WOULD LIKE TO PLACE AN ORDER.

WHAT WOULD YOU LIKE?
I TAKE ORDERS FOR EVERYDAY ITEMS ONLY.

PATHETICALLY WEAK. NOT JUST IN BODY, BUT IN MY HEART AND SOUL AS WELL.
I KNOW NOW THAT I AM WEAK.
I WANT A SWORD LIKE YOURS!
SO I WANT ONE.
I NEED A "HEART" THAT CANNOT BREAK.
I WANT YOU TO SEE ME!
FWOOSH
FOLD.

BRUSH THE SLEEP FROM YOUR EYES.
REACH FOR THE TRUTH.
HOLD THE WIND IN THESE HANDS.
CUT POINT. BLADE CONSTRUCTION: FINAL STAGE. ROUGH FINISH.
CORE STEEL, COMPLETE. SKIN STEEL, COMPLETE. BLADE CONSTRUCTION: DRAW.
CLAY COAT. HEAT. STRAIGHTEN.
FWOOOSH
SHARPEN.
FOUNDATION POLISH: BINSUI STONE. KAISEI STONE.
CHU-NAGURA STONE. KOMA-NAGURA STONE. UCHIGOMORI-STONE. FINAL POLISH...

FWOOOOOSH
JIZUYA STONE.
NUGUI. HADORI FINISH.
MIRROR POLISH. TIP POLISH.
MOUNT HILT.
KILL GOD.

The Sacred Blacksmith
聖剣の刀鍛冶
ブラックスミス

He who would forge the
"Sacred Sword." She who
would be its "sheath."

With their meeting,
the wheels of Fate have
begun to turn.

The Sacred Blacksmith

聖剣の刀鍛冶（ブラックスミス）

NEXT TIME...

聖剣の刀鍛冶
The Sacred Blacksmith
2
story: ISAO MIURA
art: KOTARO YAMADA

FROM THE STUDIO THAT BROUGHT YOU SAMURAI CHAMPLOO AND ERGO PROXY!

The Sacred Blacksmith
聖剣の刀鍛冶

THE COMPLETE SERIES
12 EPISODES ON 2 DISCS

WIELDING HIS BLADE,
SHE WILL DEFEND
THE WEAK.

OWN IT NOW ON DVD!

YOU SHOULD BE WATCHING
FUNIMATION.COM/THE-SACRED-BLACKSMITH

© 2009 Isao Miura / MEDIA FACTORY, EARTH STAR ENTERTAINMENT, JOQR, AT-X. Licensed by FUNimation® Productions, Ltd. All Rights Reserved.

Haganai
I don't have many friends
DON'T MISS THE MANGA SERIES THAT ALL THE GEEKS ARE TALKING ABOUT!
(With their imaginary friends.)
Haganai: I Don't Have Many Friends © 2010 Itachi, © 2010 Yomi Hirasaka

MAYO CHIKI!
ARE YOU NORMAL? THIS MANGA IS DEFINITELY NOT!
P.S. CHECK OUT THE ANIME FROM SENTAI FILMWORKS!
Mayo Chiki! © 2010 Neet, © 2010 Hajime Asano

TO ALL CREATURES OF THE NIGHT:
YOUR SALVATION HAS ARRIVED!

DANCE IN THE VAMPIRE BUND © 2006 NOZOMU TAMAKI

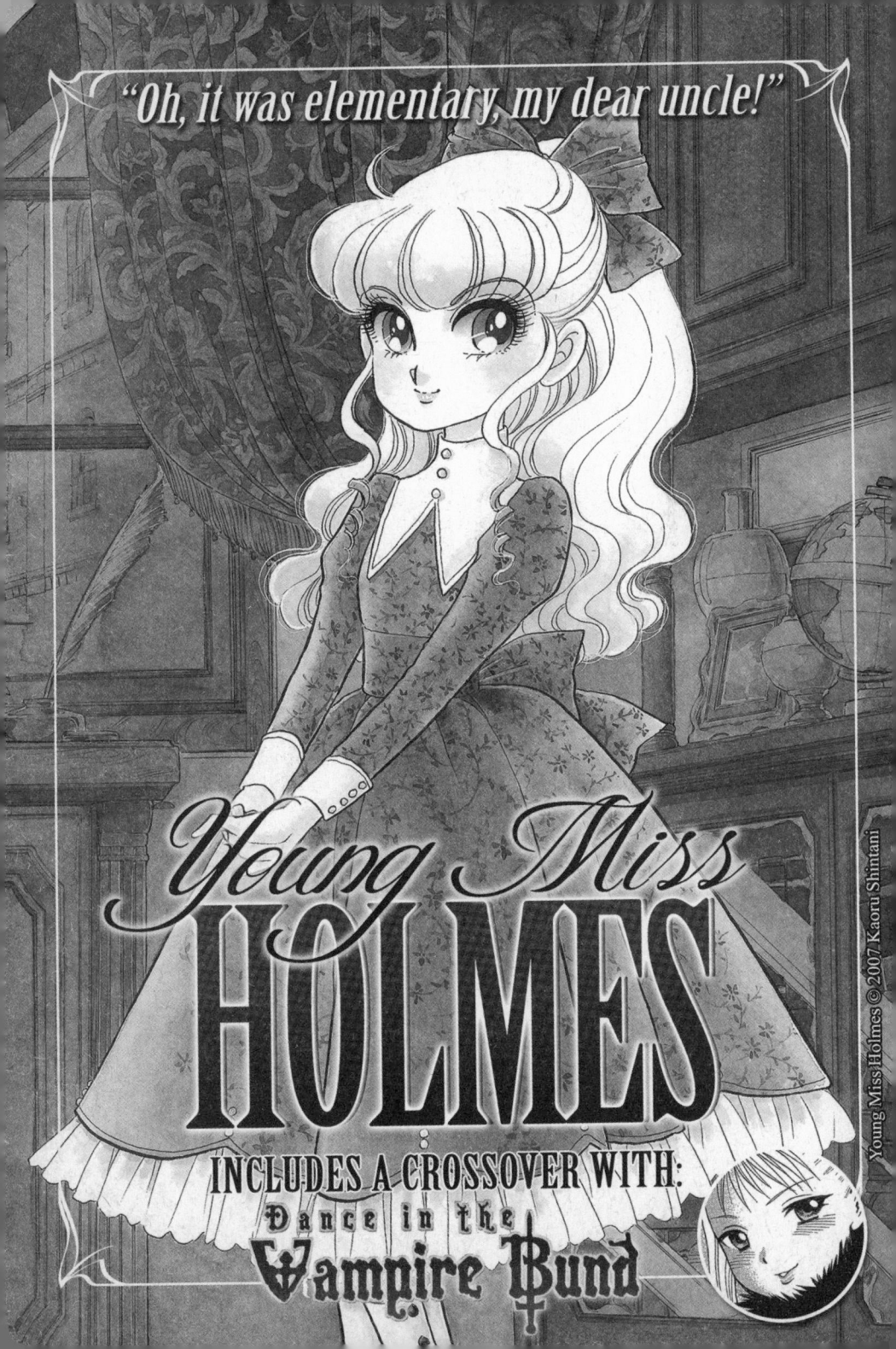
"Oh, it was elementary, my dear uncle!"
Young Miss HOLMES
INCLUDES A CROSSOVER WITH:
Dance in the Vampire Bund
Young Miss Holmes © 2007 Kaoru Shintani

WWW.ZOOMCOMICS.COM
READ FREE ONLINE COMICS!
ZOOM COMICS
Home to free webcomics from Seven Seas Entertainment!
WWW.ZOOMCOMICS.COM

Experience all that SEVEN SEAS has to offer!

Visit us Online and follow us on Twitter!

WWW.GOMANGA.COM

WWW.TWITTER.COM/GOMANGA

STAFF CREDITS

translation **Adrienne Beck**
adaptation **Janet Houck**
lettering **Roland Amago**
layout **Bambi Eloriaga-Amago**
cover design **Nicky Lim**
copy editor **Shanti Whitesides**
editor **Adam Arnold**

publisher **Jason DeAngelis**
Seven Seas Entertainment

THE SACRED BLACKSMITH VOLUME 1
Copyright © 2009 Kotaro Yamada, Isao Miura / MEDIA FACTORY
First published in Japan in 2009 by MEDIA FACTORY, Inc.
English translation rights reserved by Seven Seas Entertainment, LLC. under the license from MEDIA FACTORY, Inc., Tokyo, Japan.

No portion of this book may be reproduced or transmitted in any form without written permission from the copyright holders. This is a work of fiction. Names, characters, places, and incidents are the products of the author's imagination or are used fictitiously. Any resemblance to actual events, locales, or persons, living or dead, is entirely coincidental.

Seven Seas and the Seven Seas logo are trademarks of Seven Seas Entertainment, LLC. All rights reserved.

ISBN: 978-1-937867-32-4

Printed in Canada

First Printing: May 2013

10 9 8 7 6 5 4 3 2 1

FOLLOW US ONLINE: ***www.gomanga.com***

READING DIRECTIONS

This book reads from ***right to left***, Japanese style. If this is your first time reading manga, you start reading from the top right panel on each page and take it from there. If you get lost, just follow the numbered diagram here. It may seem backwards at first, but you'll get the hang of it! Have fun!!